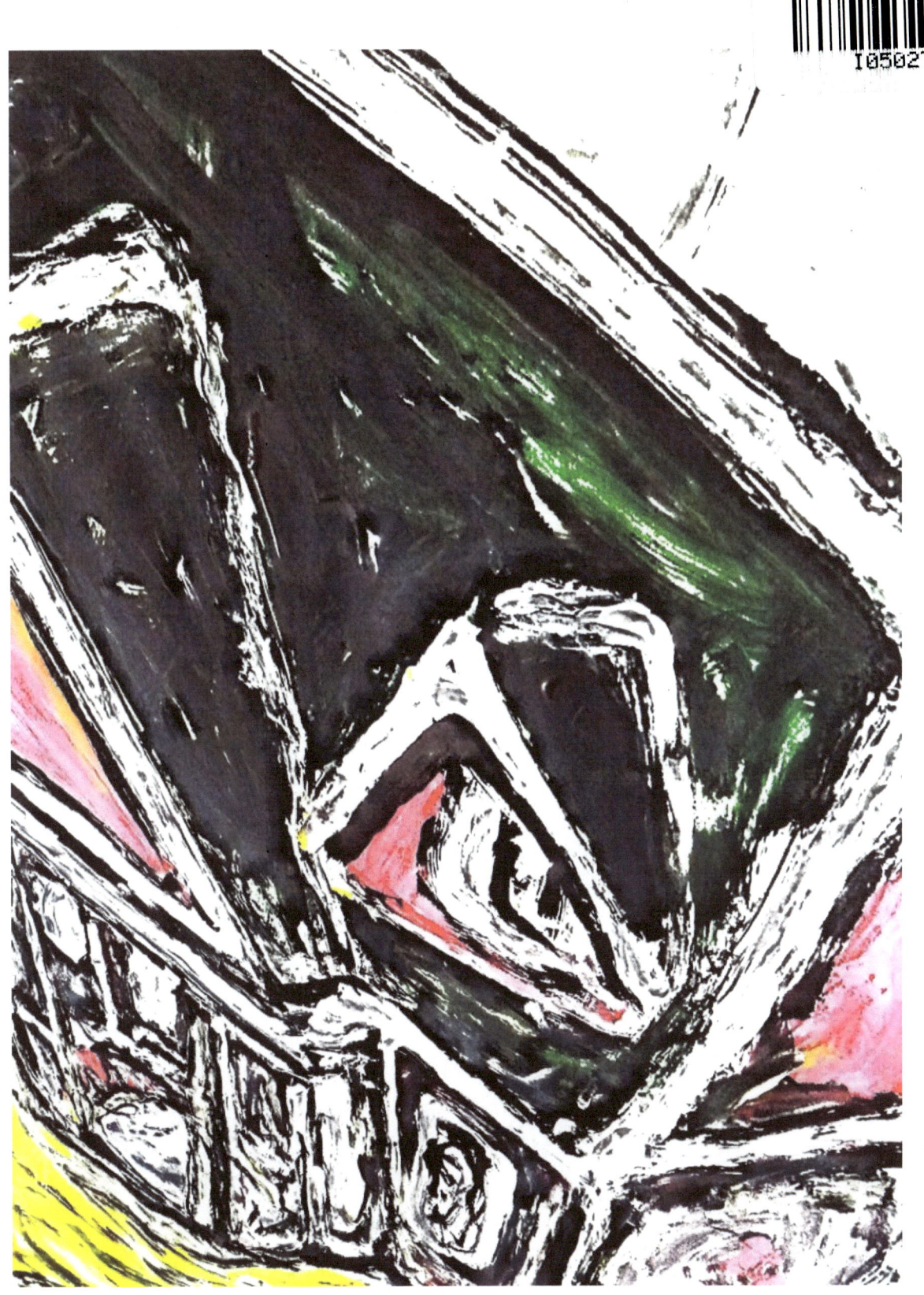

re-manipulations: images and poetry altered to tell a tale

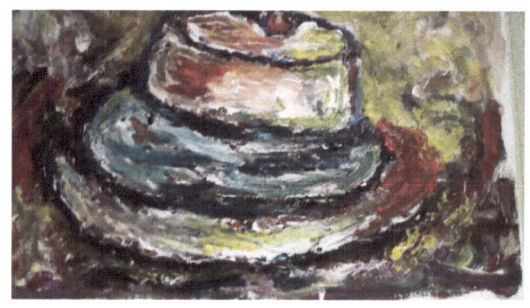

a book of images and words

images and text by Patrick B. Humphreys

introduction

this is a different book for me. In the past I have made books that feature only visual elements or a book with only words such as "low key supermarket free verse", America Star Books, ISBN: 978-1142629787, 2011 . The rest of the books I have had published on CreateSpace are primarily visual in nature but I wanted to do something that was more than just words or pictures but that showed the complete picture. Words and images make up me , the true me . This books illustrates the true me : words and images together.

Re-manipulated to tell a tale. My tale. The tale that only I can tell.

With that said,

Here it is

Patrick B. Humphreys

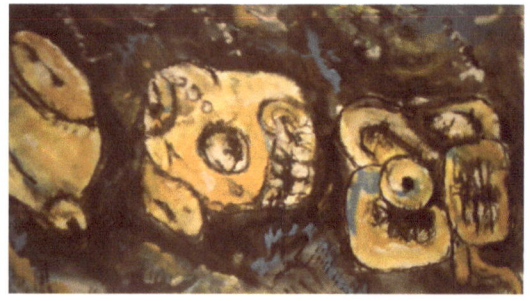

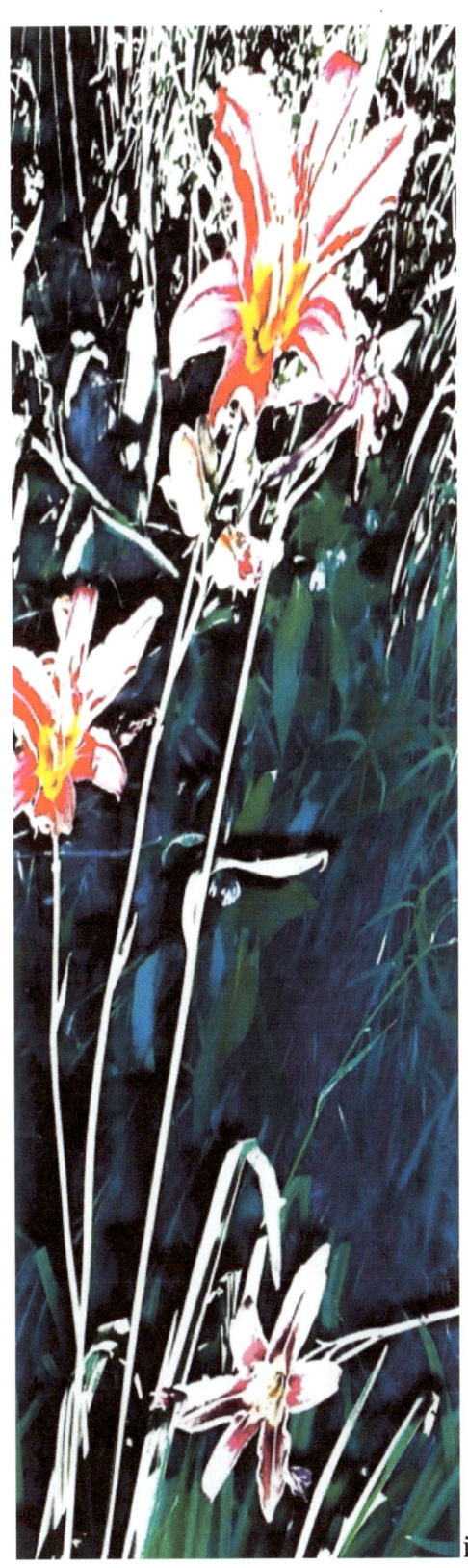

sliver

of

a

flower

is

this

it

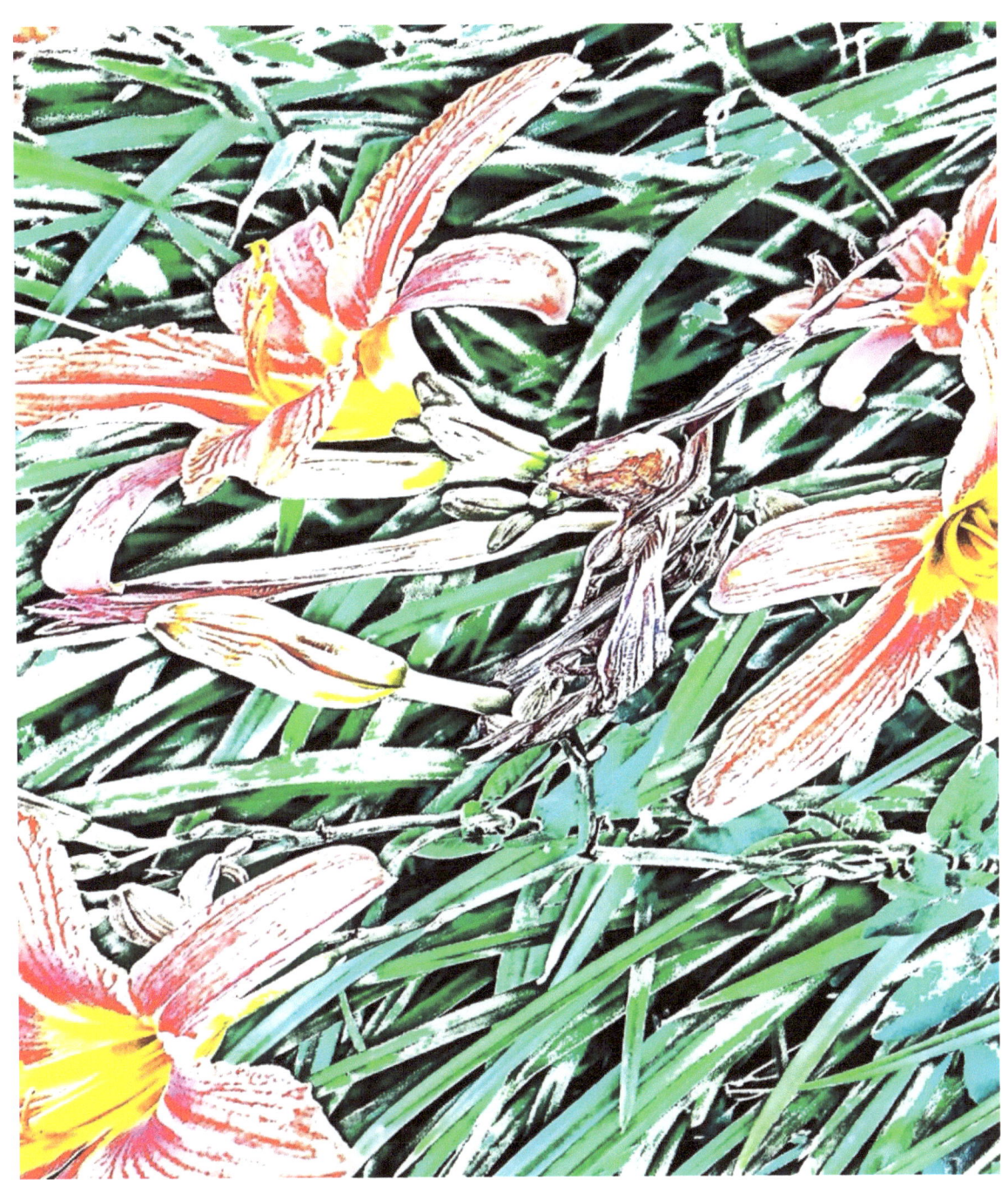

image previous
taken at dan's
tiger lilies
manipulated
colorized
energized
is that you
are you
gaudy
cool color
abstract
superhero
villain
which are
villain
truth
lies
reunion
smile
the color
does it
need
words
image alone
words
alone
together
better
image previous

Pink houses
Discarded
Found at
Flea market
Manipulated with
Phone

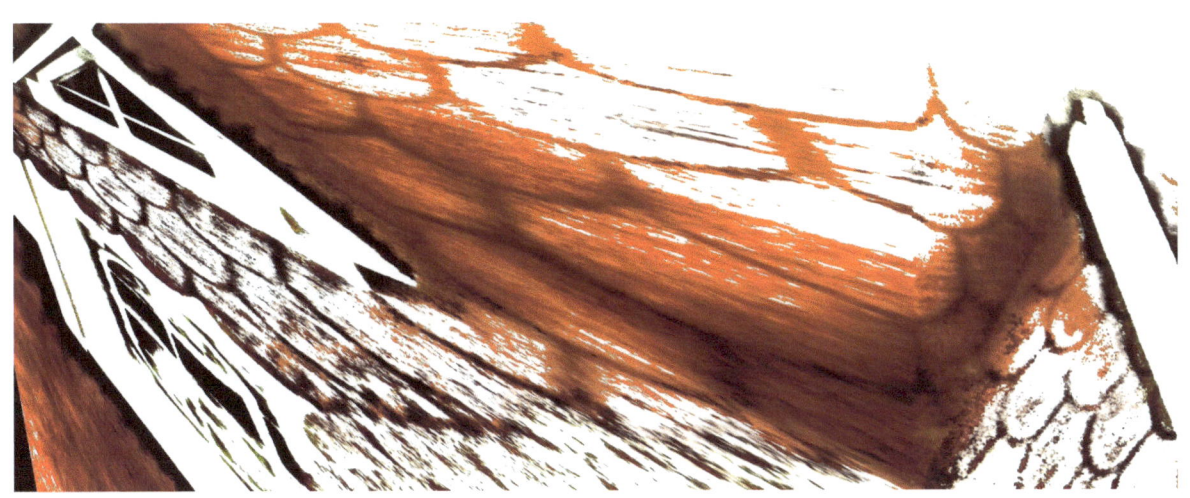

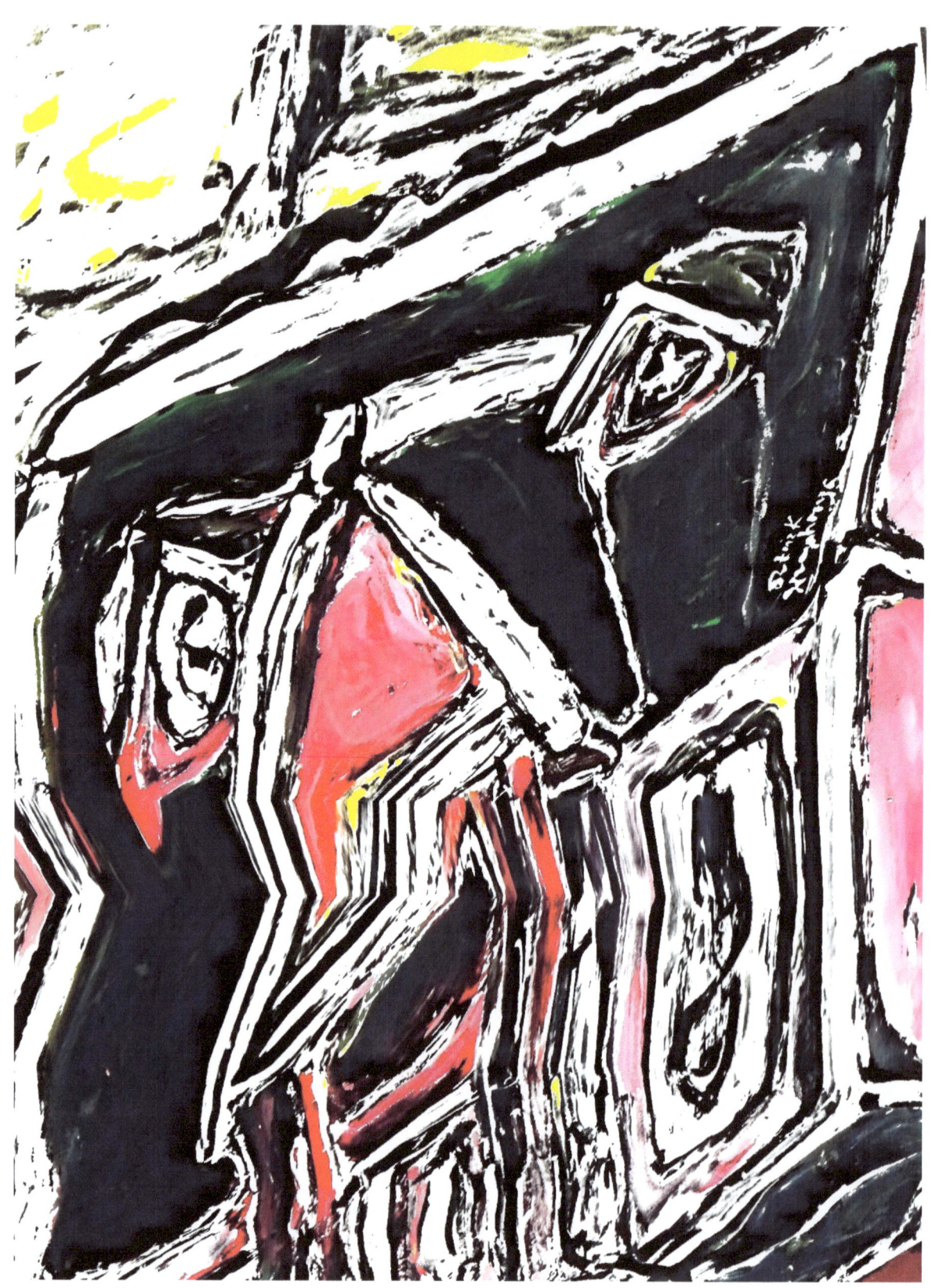

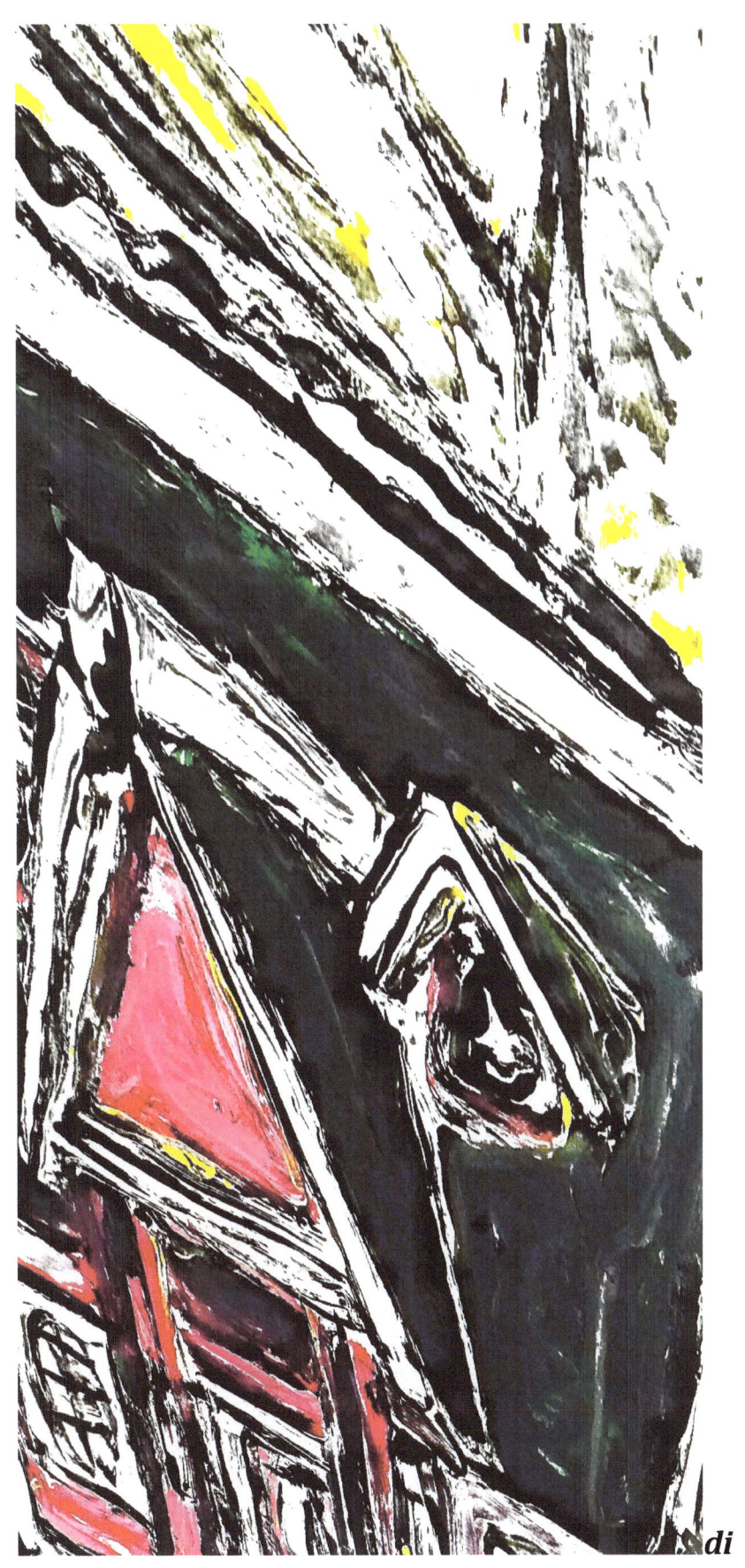

DISTORT
IONS
IS
THIS
RIGHT
WRONG
WHO KNOWS
WHO DECIDES
TRUTH
;I\LIES
DISTORT
MY EYES
VISION
LIES
TRUTH
YOUR VIEW
NOT MINE
DISTORT
IONS

MINE
MINE
ALONE
I DON'T
WANT
IT
TELL ME
LIES
EASE MY
DESIRES
FULFILL
MY
FANTASIES
DISTORT
IONS
DISTORT

DISTORT

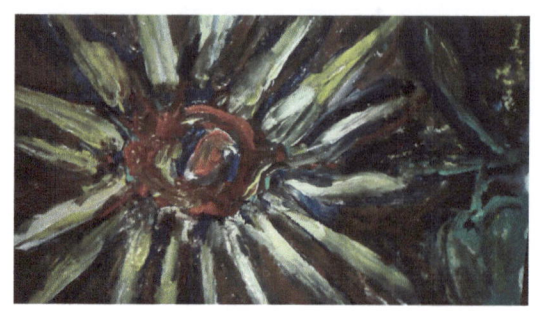

sunflowers
in a vase, in a jar
flower of the sun
van gogh, from afar
joy, reason for fun
painting of a star
flowers, two not one

see below

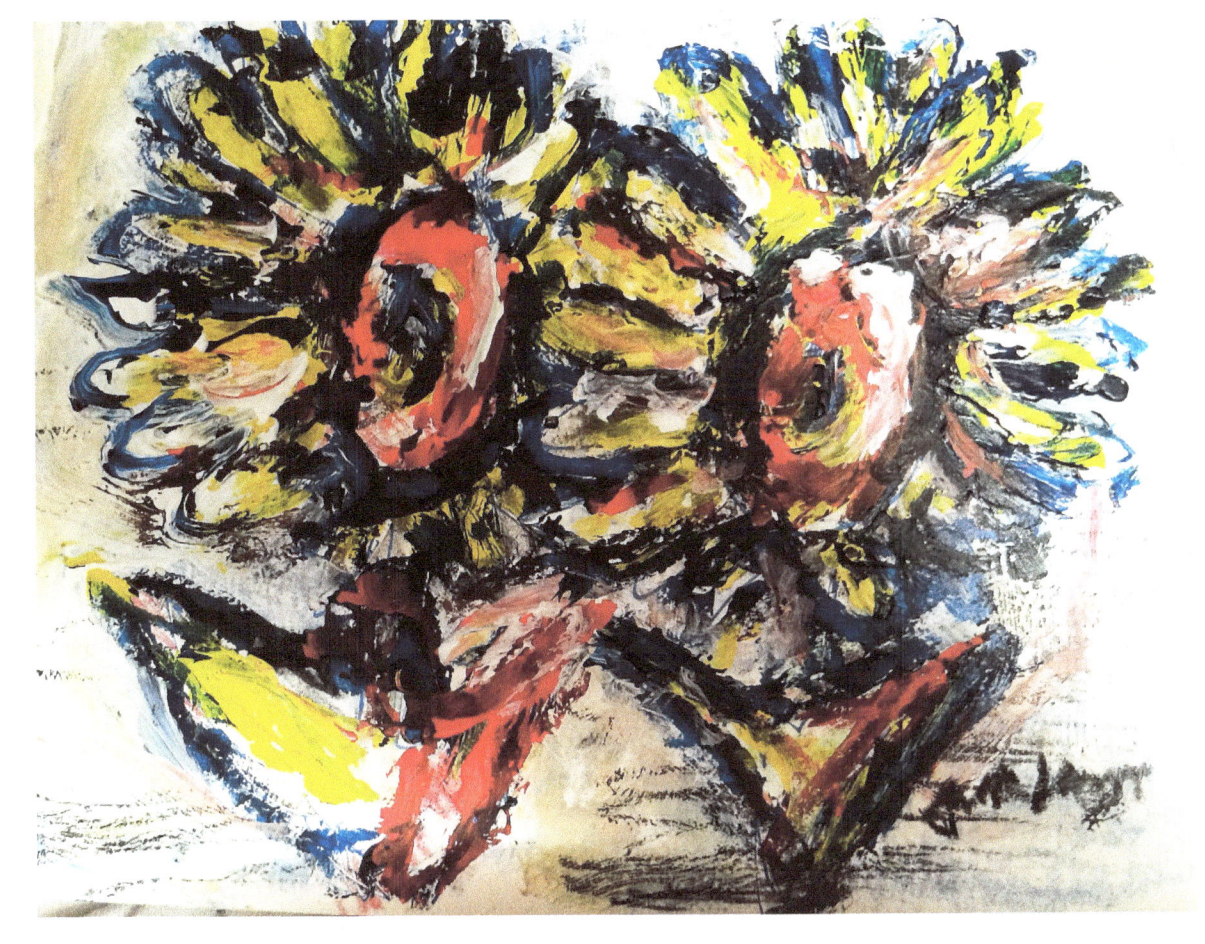

image above

poem previous

yellow tulips

light
the
sky
pondering
wondering

why
o'

why

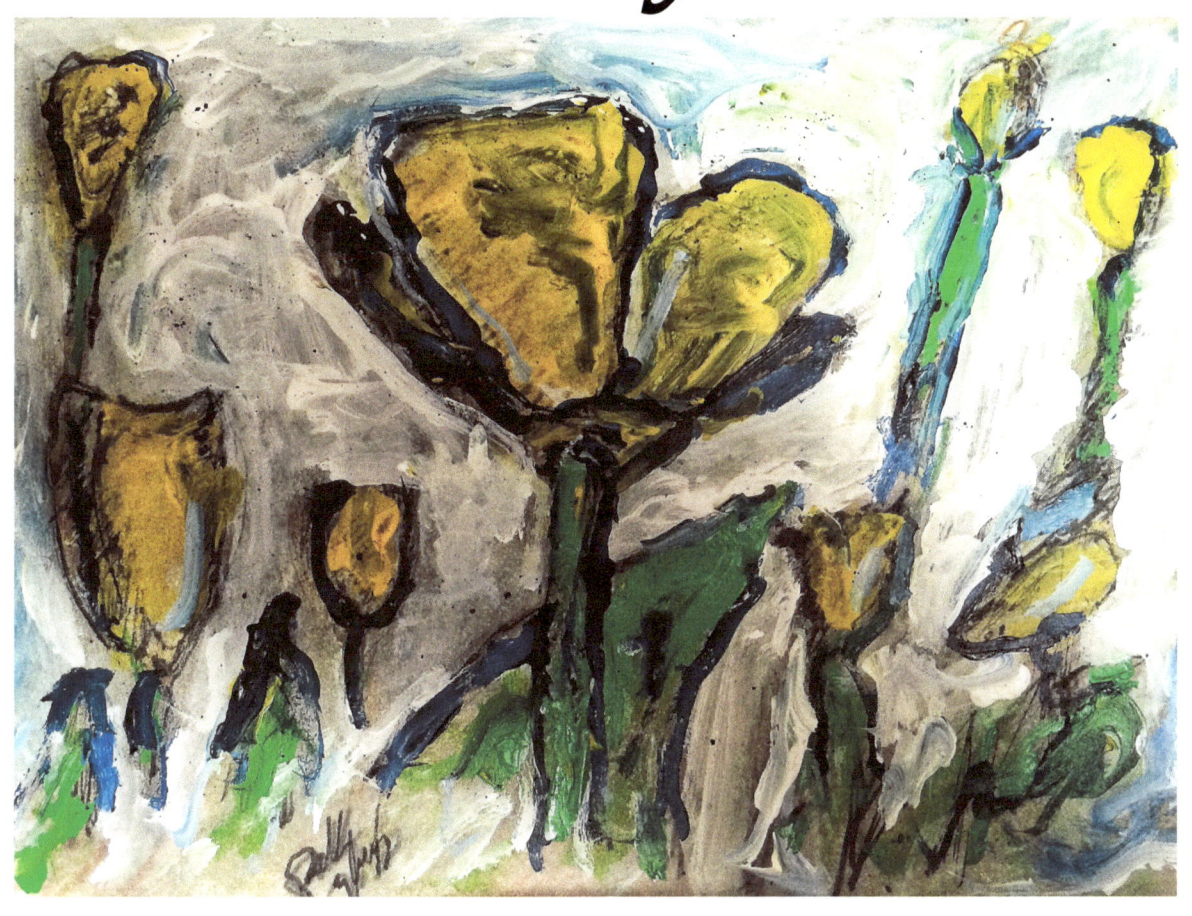

next image
next poem

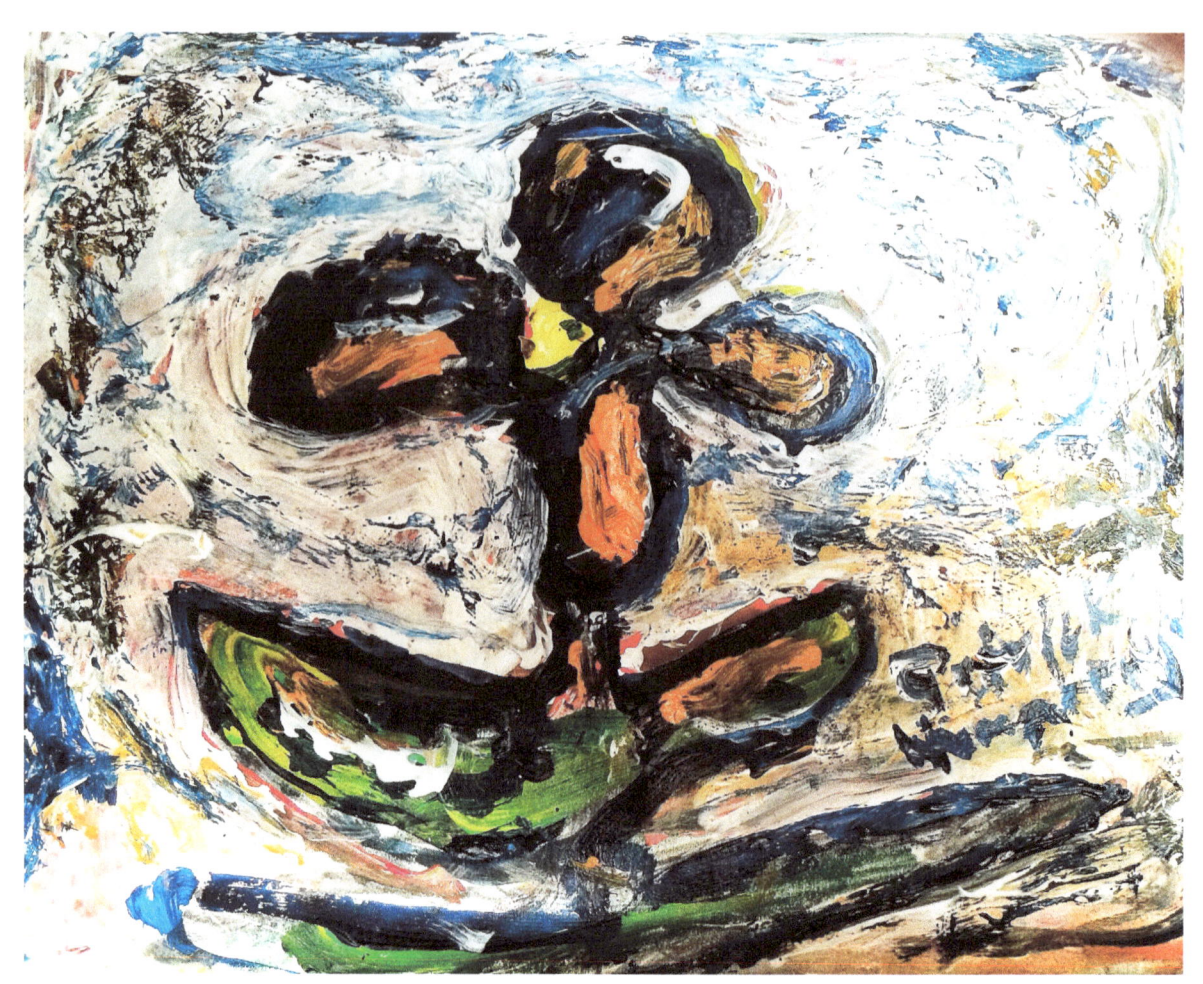

black iris

truth or

fiction

religion
faith
conviction

faith
in a
building?

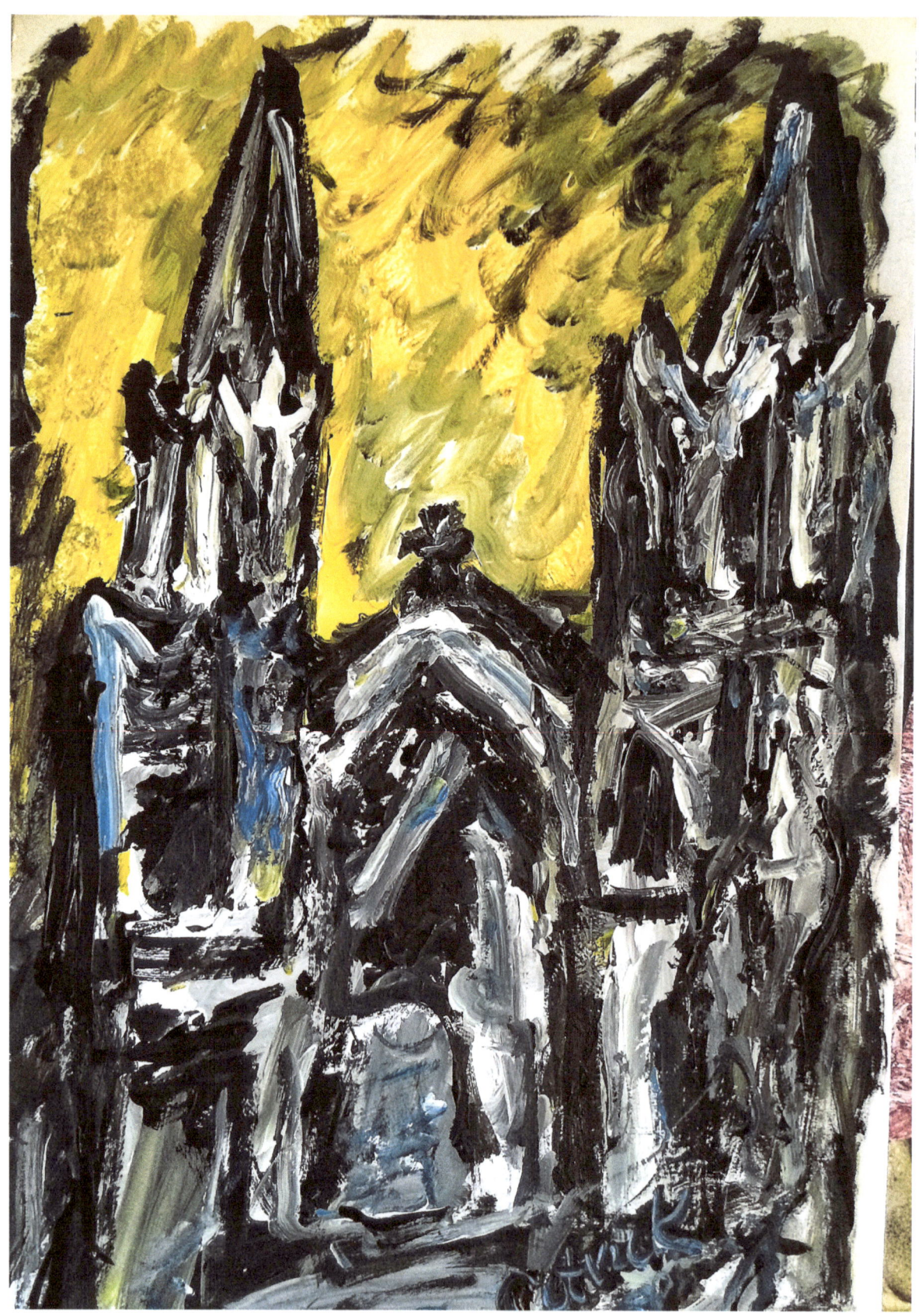

or a name?

saint stan's
our lady of
Czestochowa
?

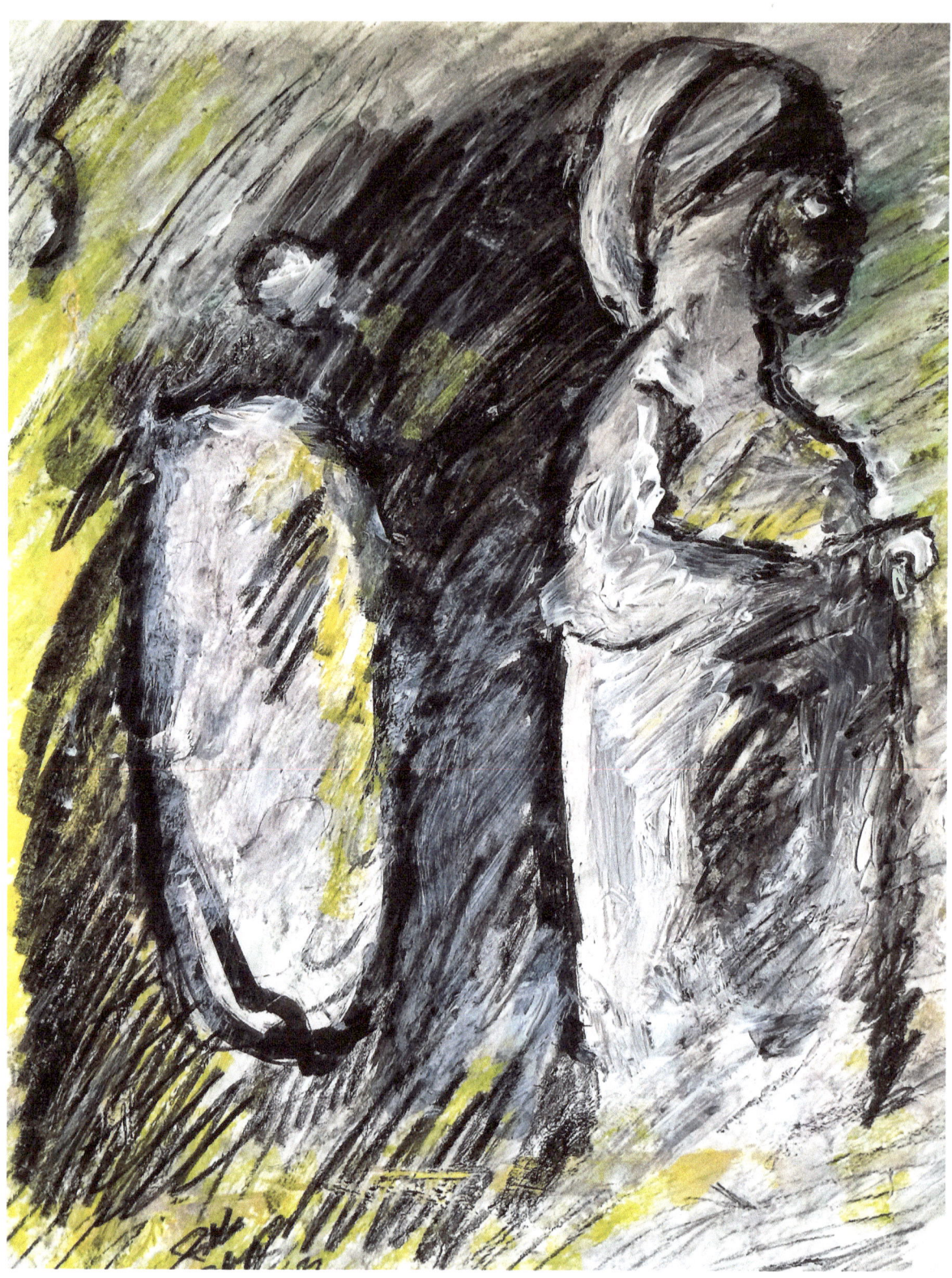

image of
MARY
one above
or
one below

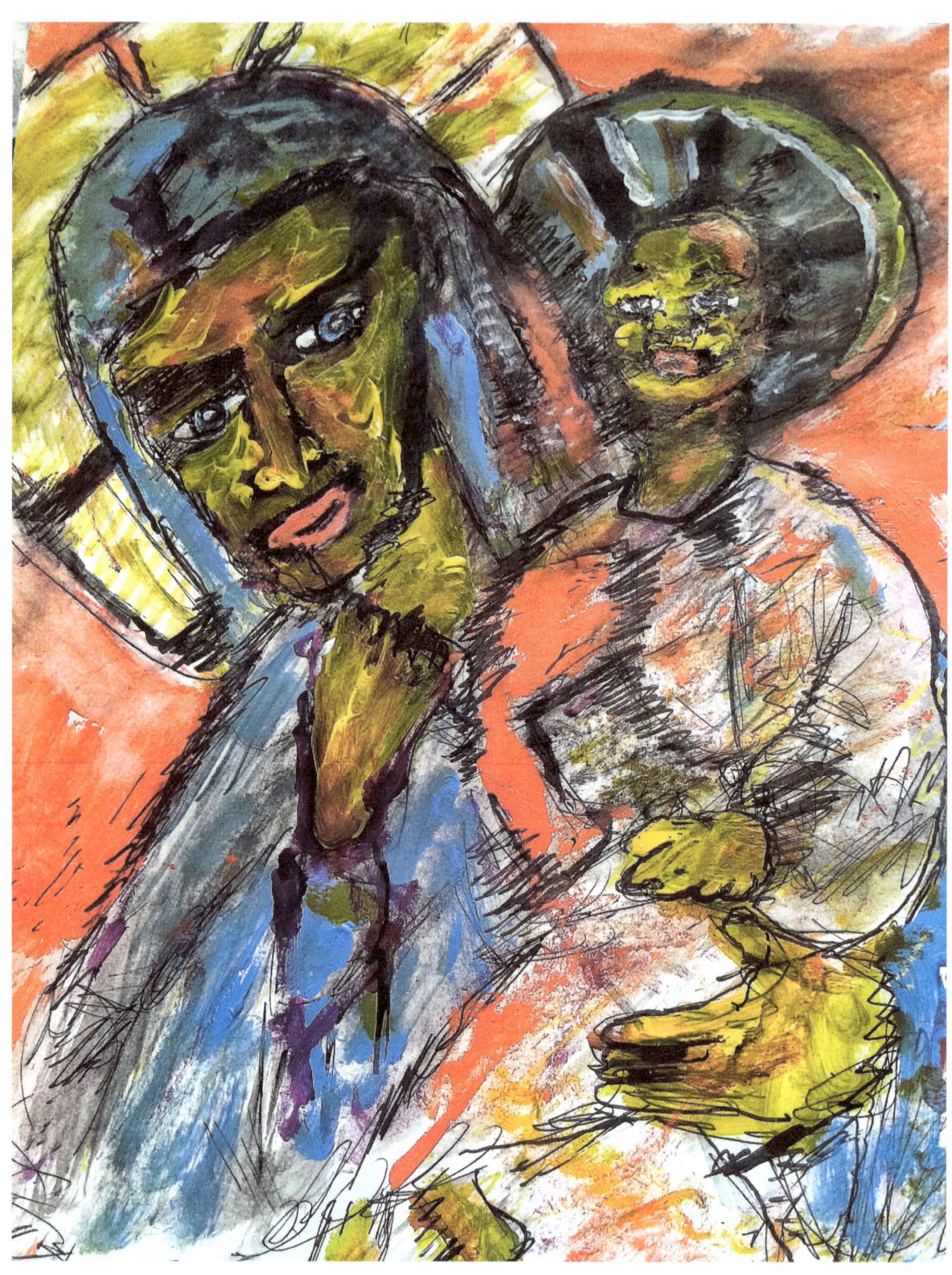

Mary
Pray for us

Flowers
Beautiful
Flowers
Poetry

Images

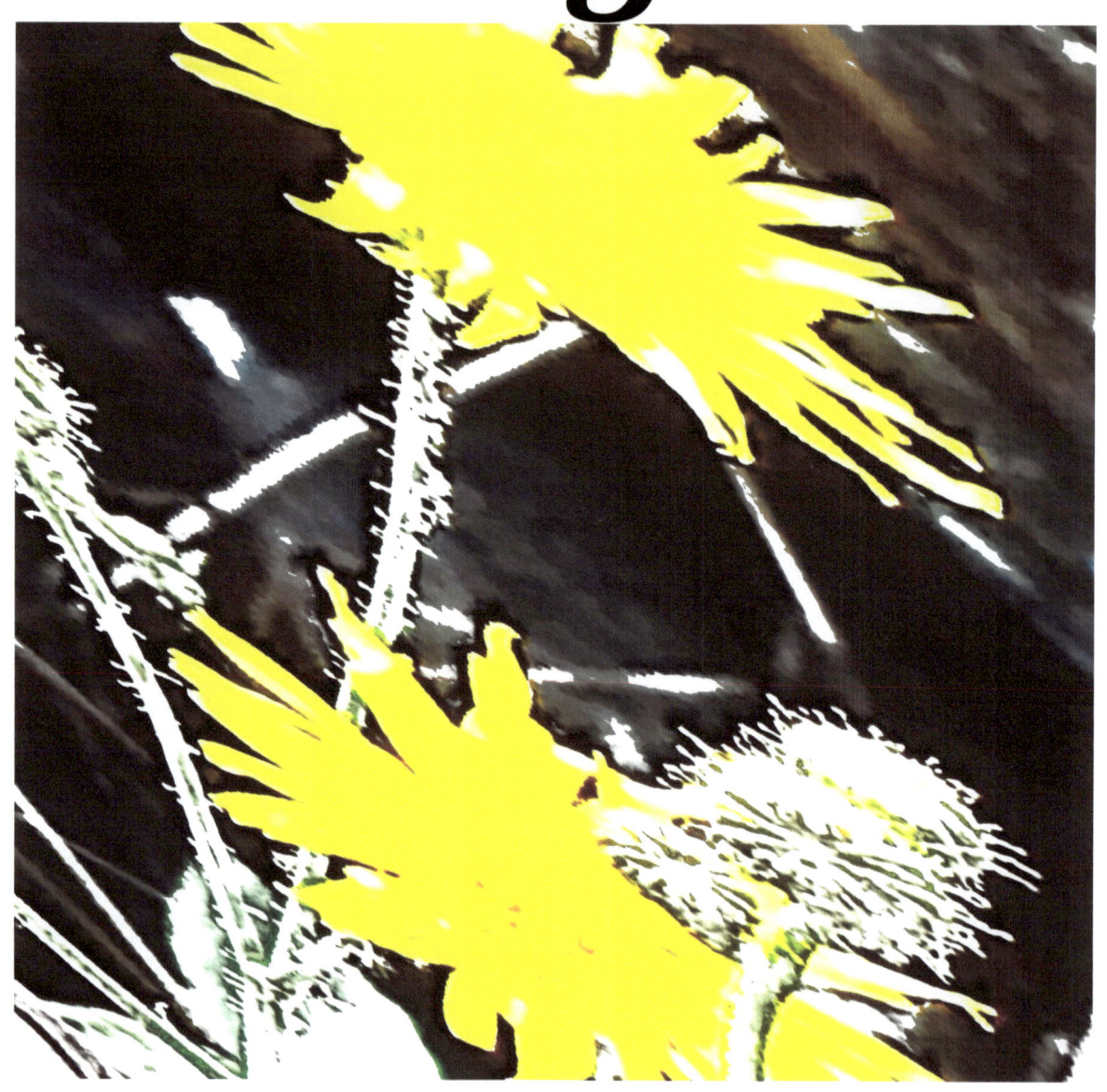

distortions

  unnatural color

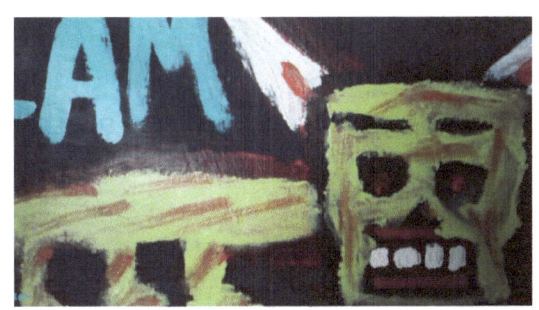

Cameron
Masterpiece

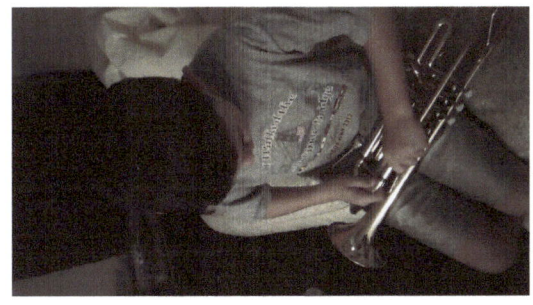

trumpet
no more

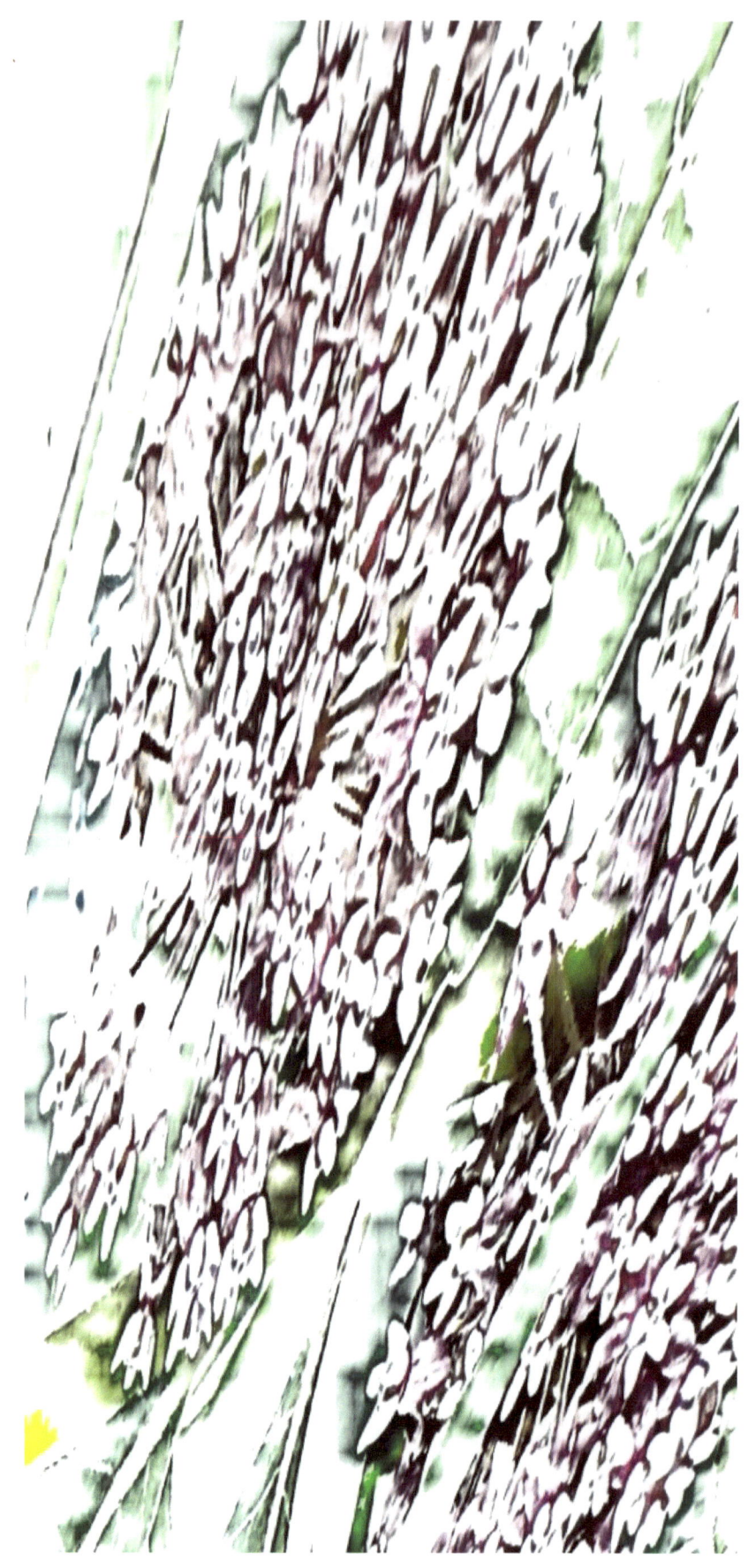

*fuchsia,   hybrid
white,   pink, summer
purple,   violet*

*bicolored, magenta
drawing below
not below
below photo
next page
yes next page
ink , watercolor pencil*

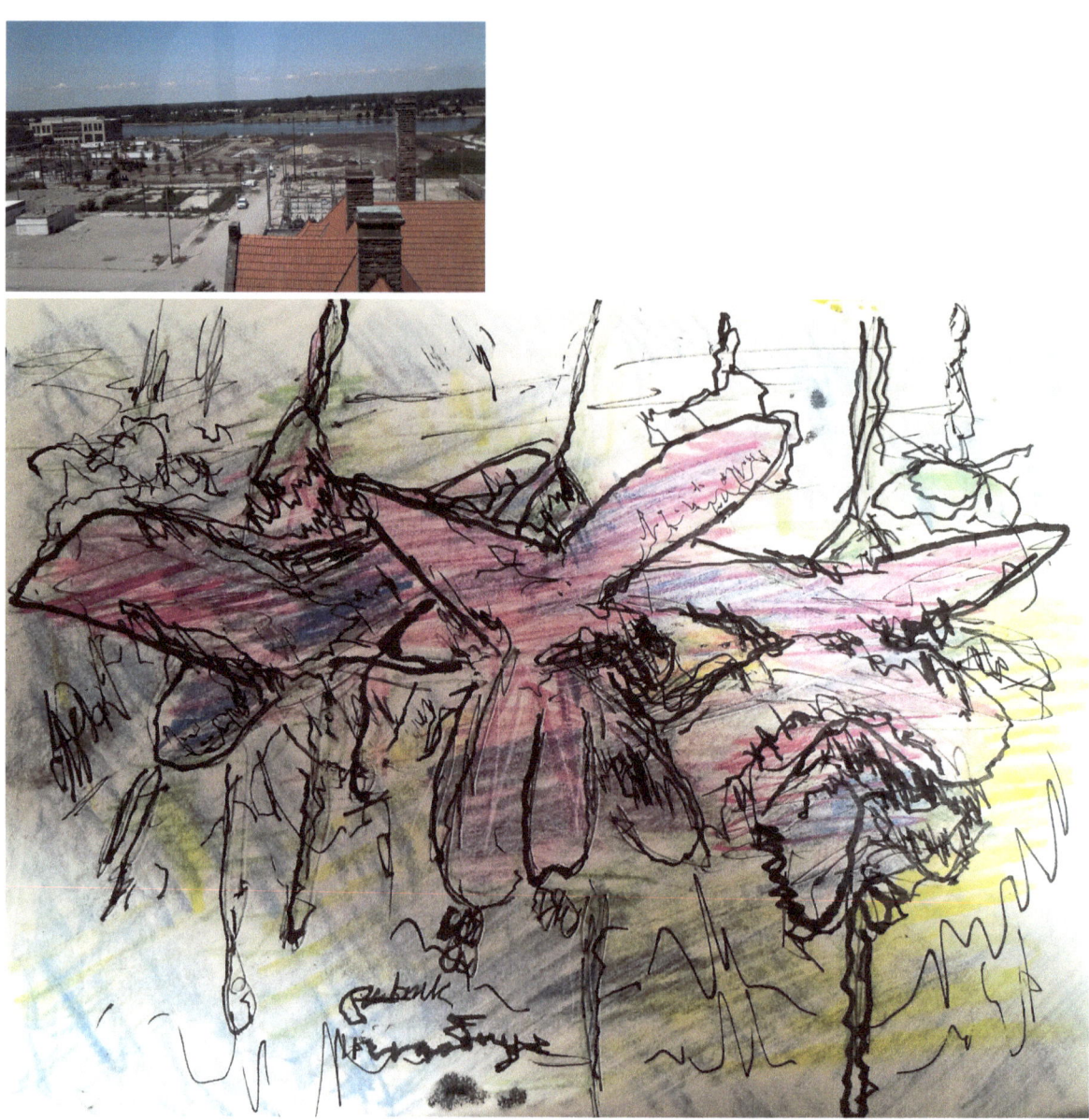

Daisy, white petals
Artist favorite, yes
Winter flower,
metals
Summer blooming,
Yes

Daisy, lover
Sensual

Be my model
Friend or lover

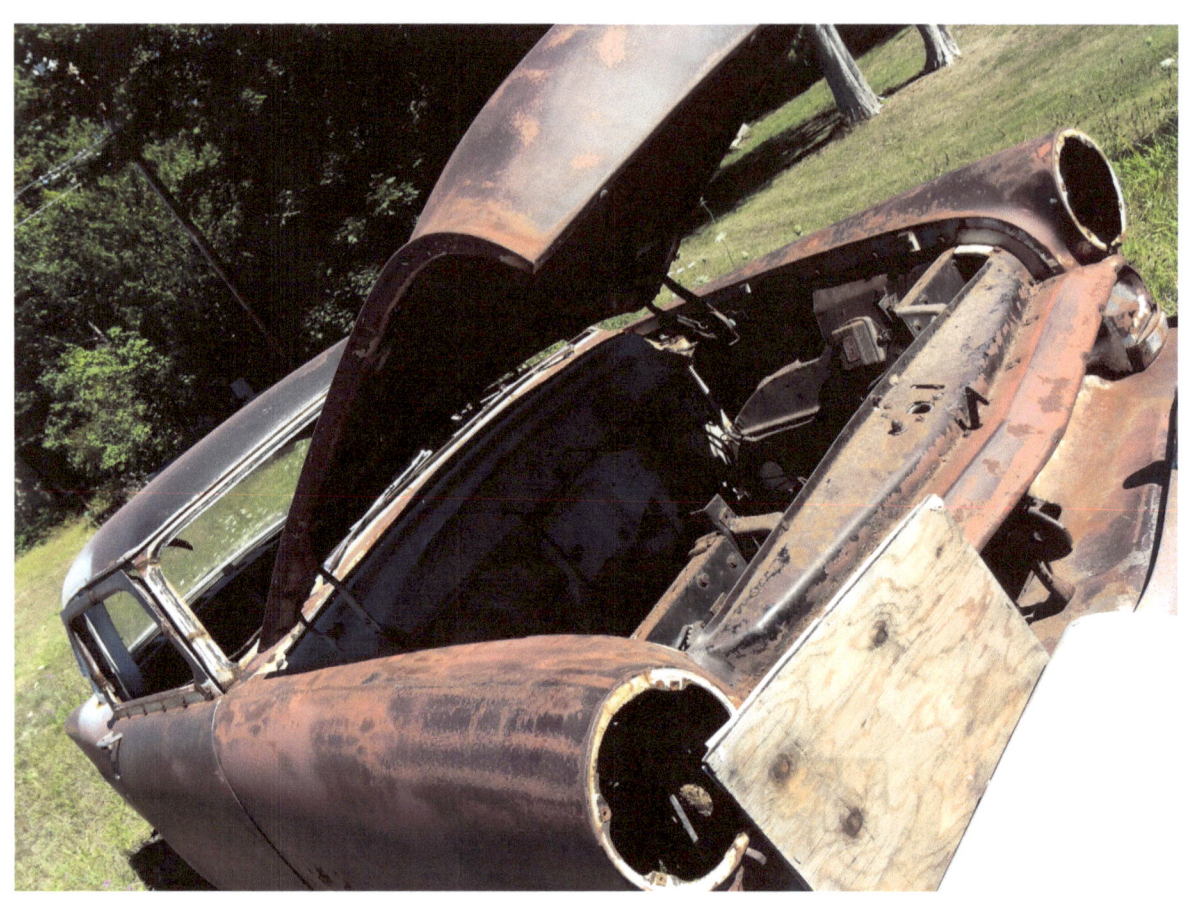

broken car

that is for sale
rusted metal
faded paint
500 dollars
lots of work
project car
not for me

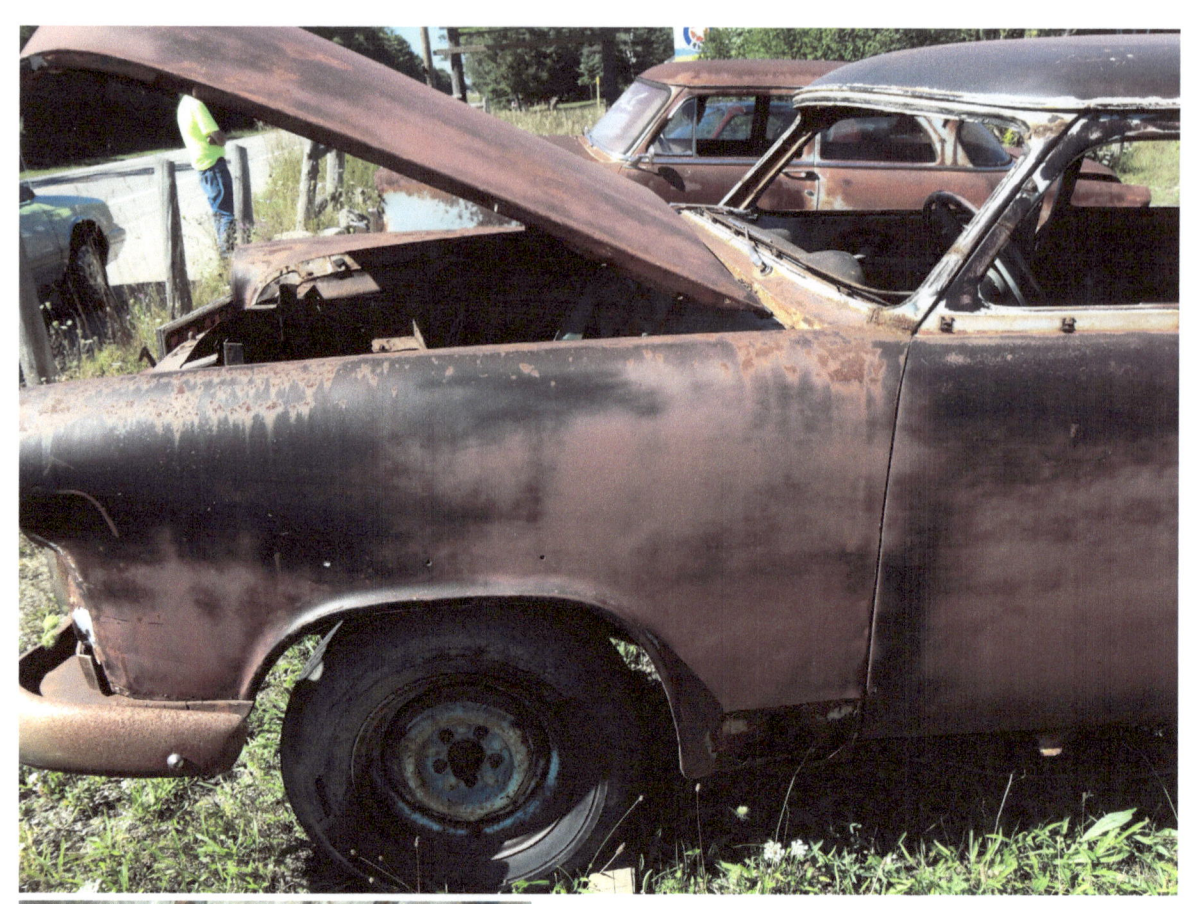

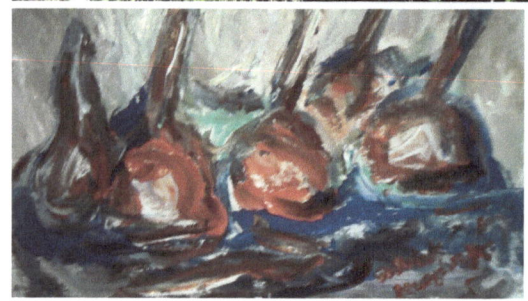

**cherries
do not [pop]
milk**

like

it

pleasure

sweet

desire

cold

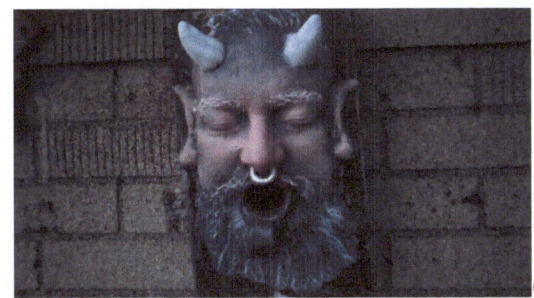

demon ?

no, it is just dan
a reflection of him

good

bad

t
  r
    u
      t
       h
        ?

lies !!
tell me why , o ' why ?

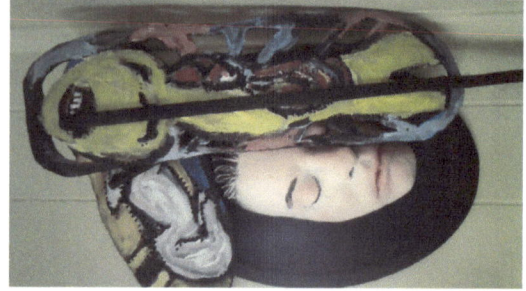

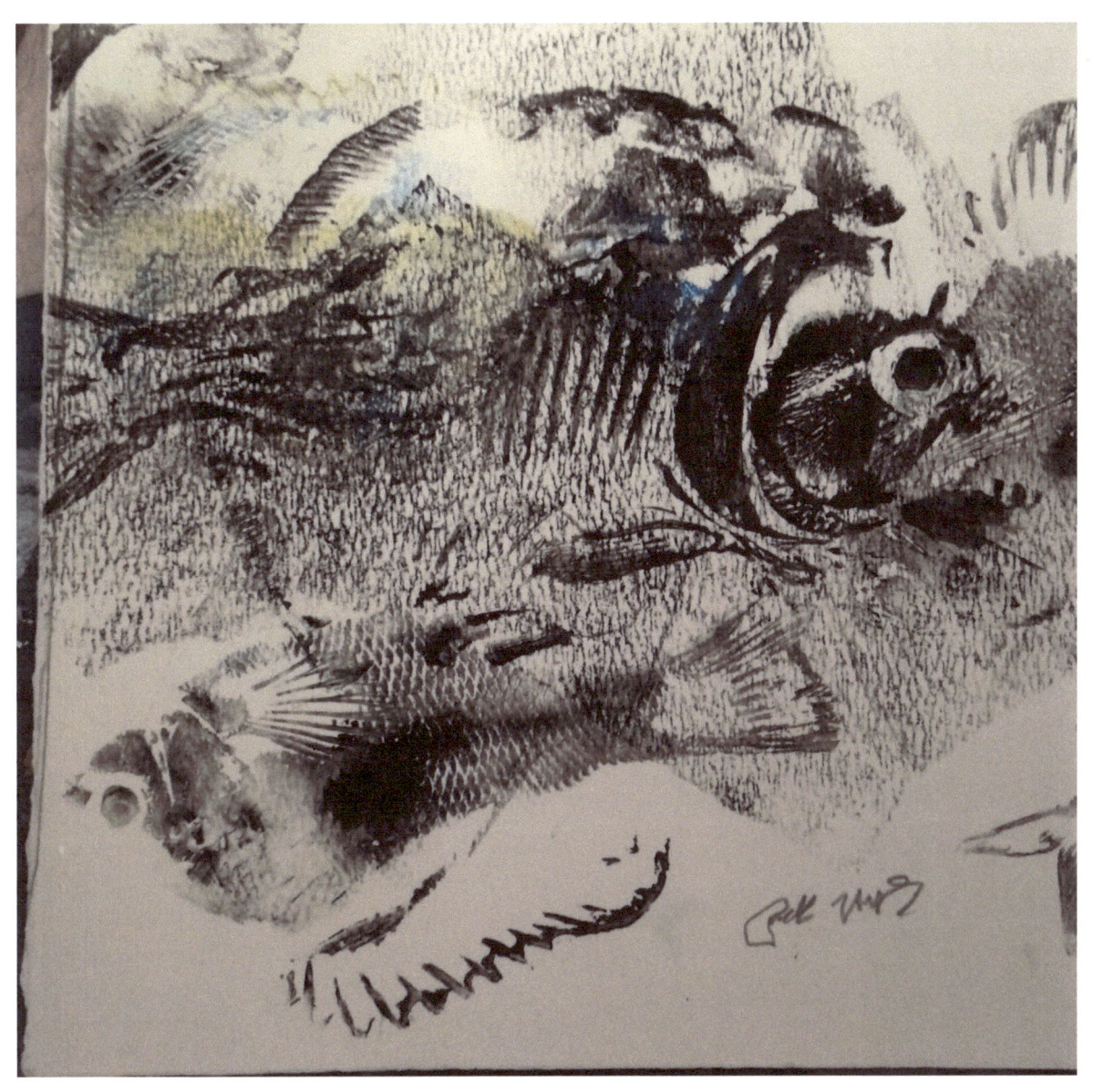

gyotabstract
my term
my image
fish print=gyotaku
+abstract paint
equals
gyotabstract

another example

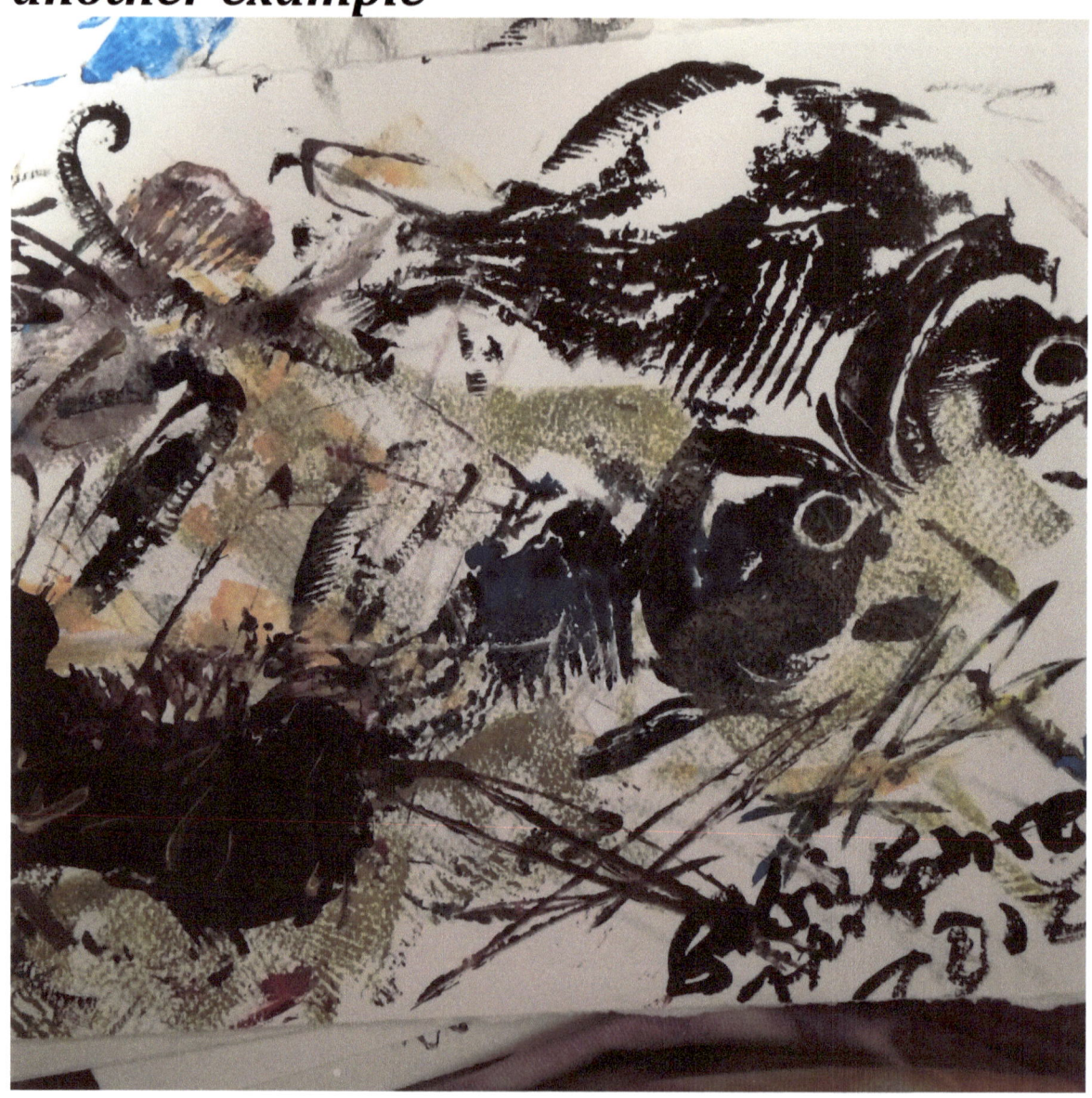

another language

mayan

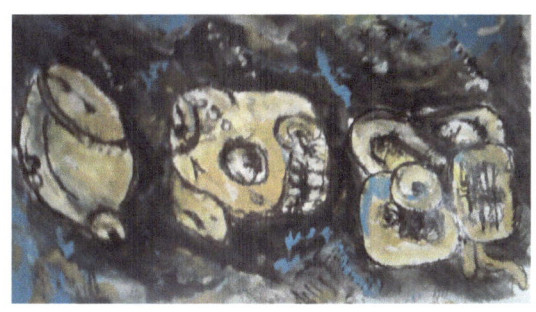

penis
turtle
?

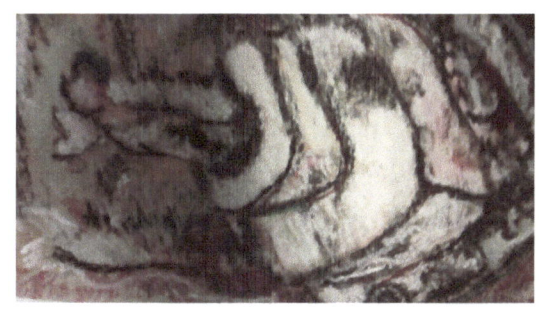

wedding cake
will I ever find love
again

before
was it
ever
never
real
forever
maybe
a baby
the
reason for
reason against

no more fighting

I am tired

Is this

It

All

Take

Give

Eat

Procreate

Ejaculate

Is it a sin

To desire
To want

What
    Is
Love
    Lust

Desire?
Greed
    A picture

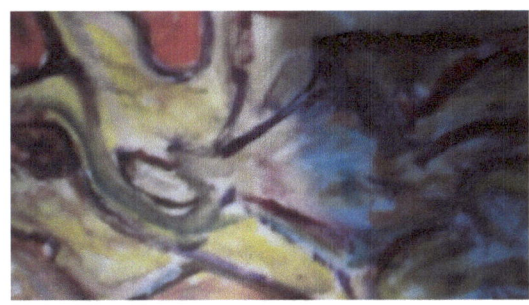

what is it
why is it small

small
      small

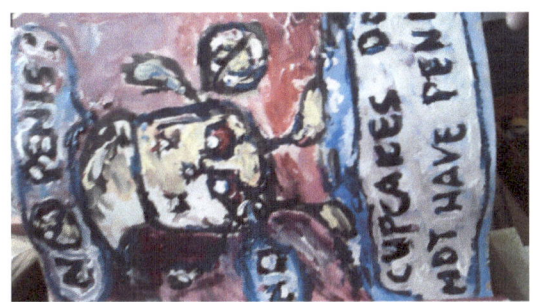

cupcakes do

not have a penis

they do not
do not
have a
penis

see illustration'
above and below

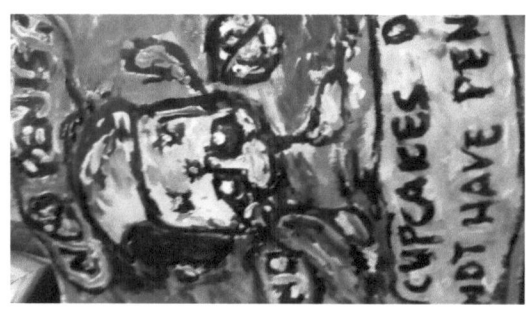

what the ?!!?? makes no sense does to me yes to me

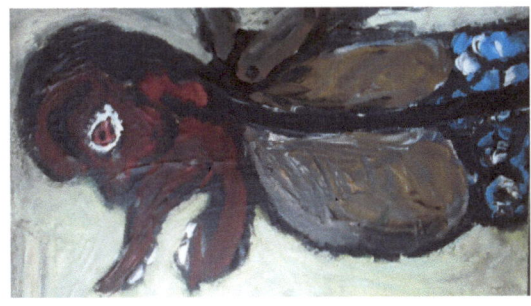

have to believe
this is hard to read

that is my point
I don't know
Where it will go I

Have to

Need to

Believe
It will be
Has to
Be

??

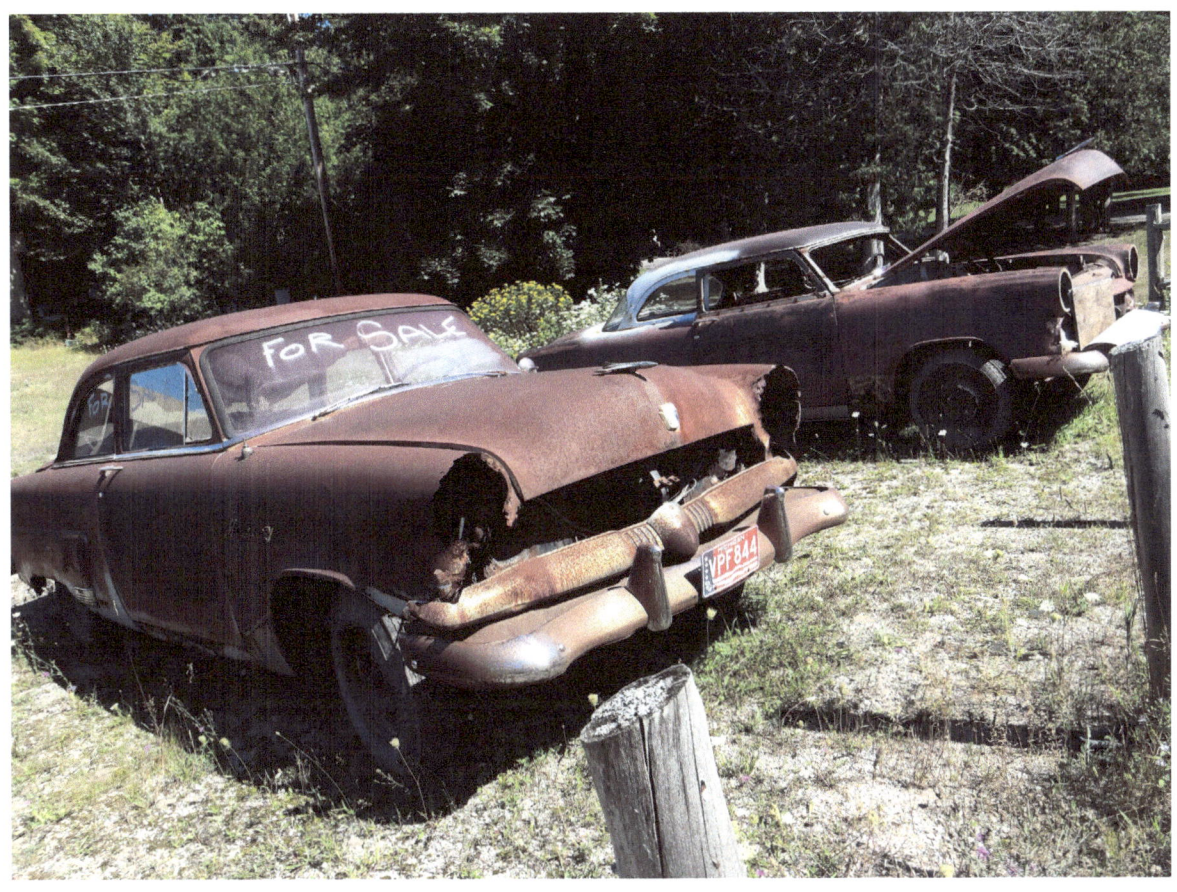

a rusted car

or two?
No I am a

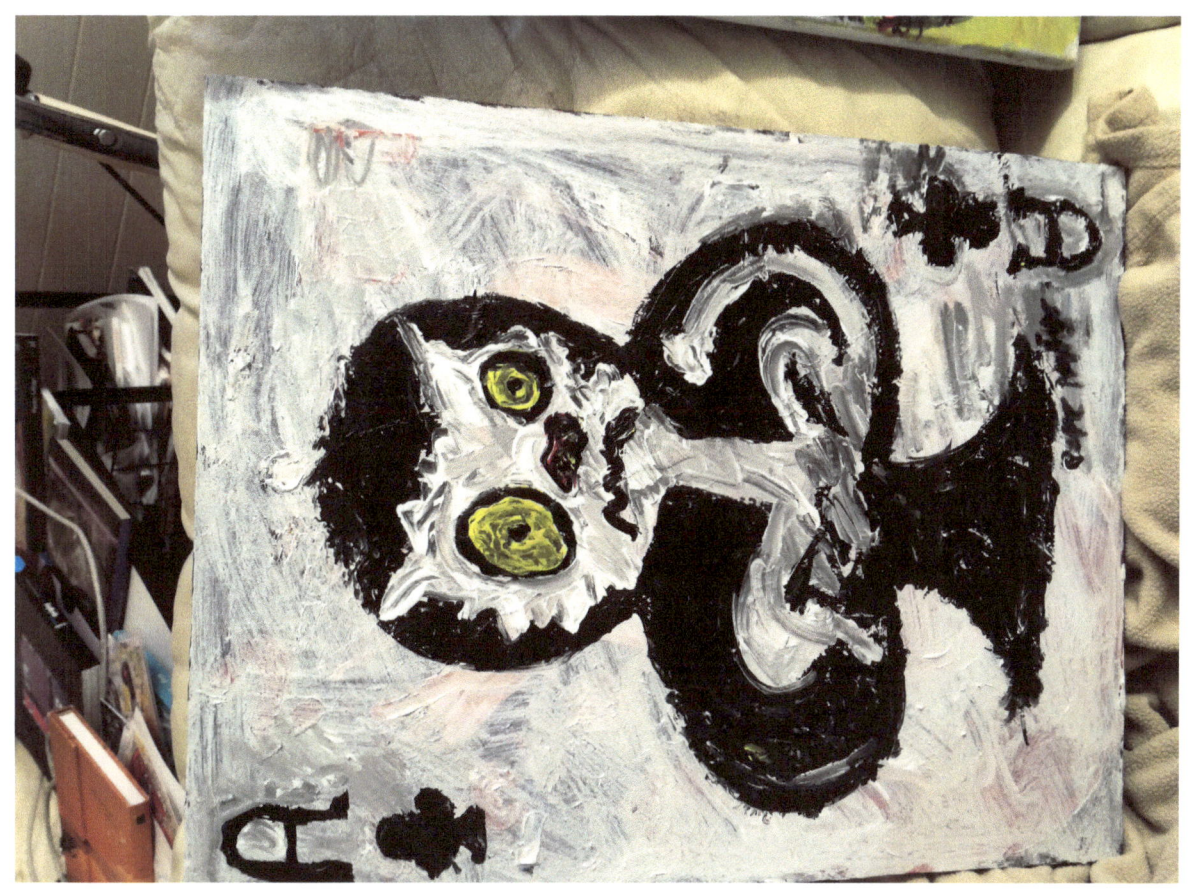

a cat playing card bad photo?

A sad kitty?

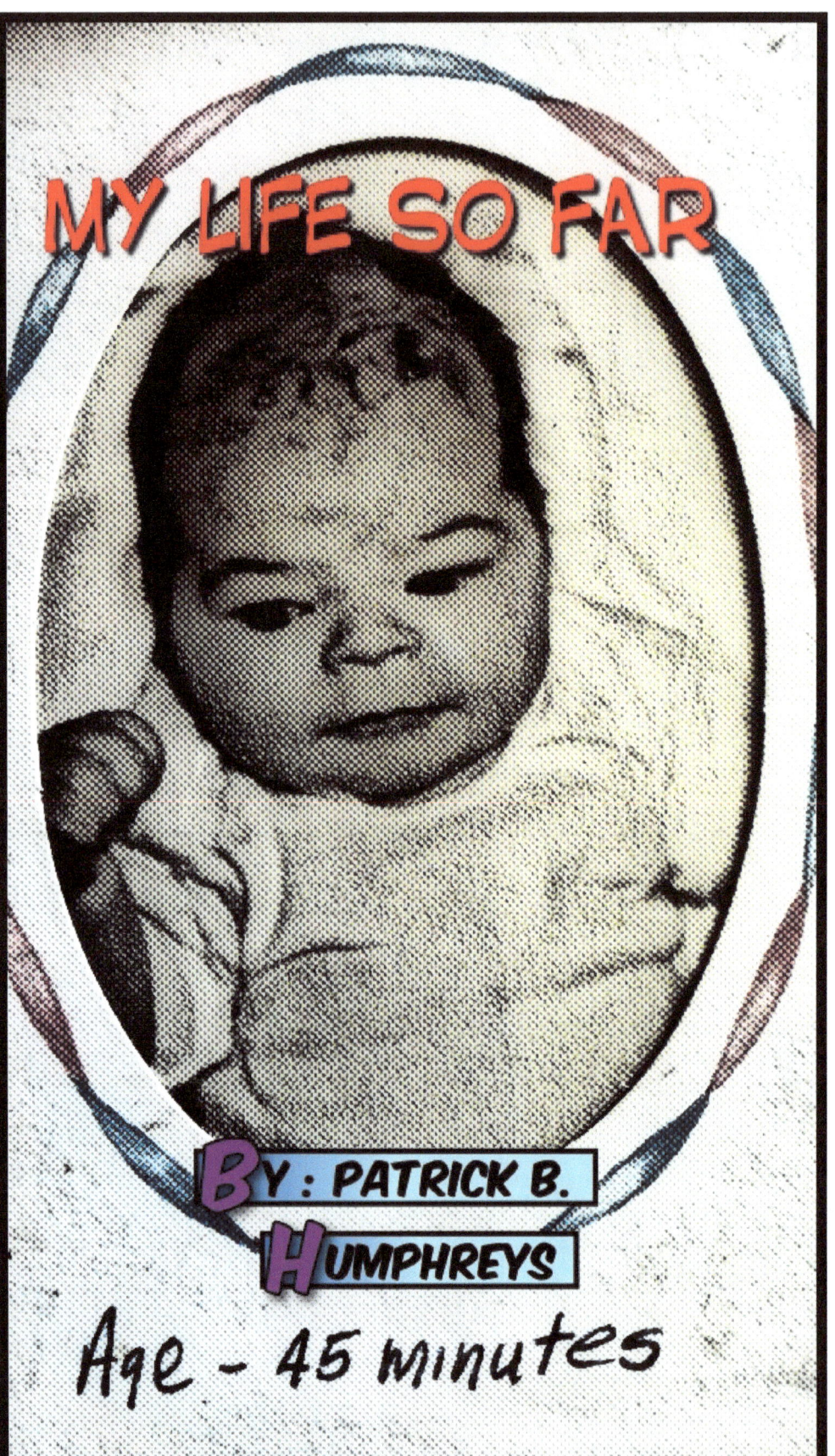

this is **what I was**
what am I now?

What will i?

Become?
Past

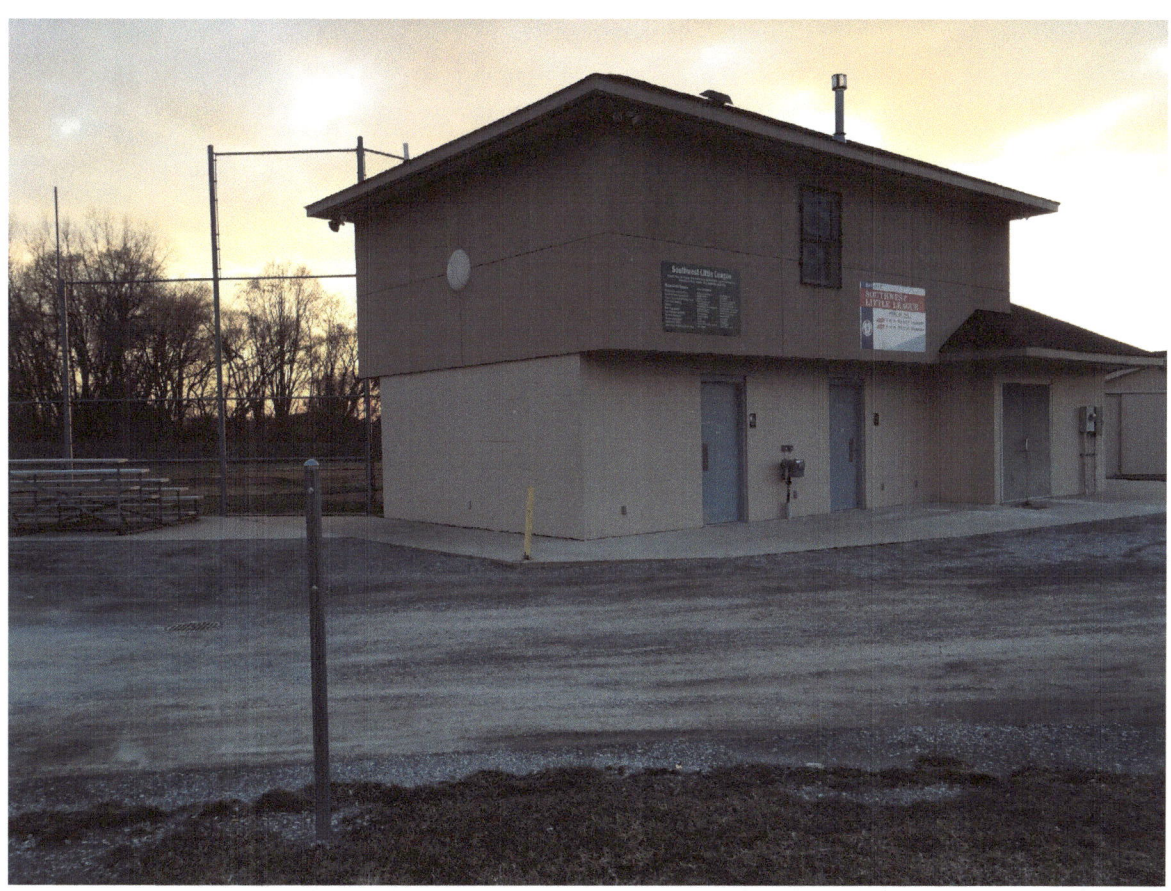

little league?

Is this the big league?

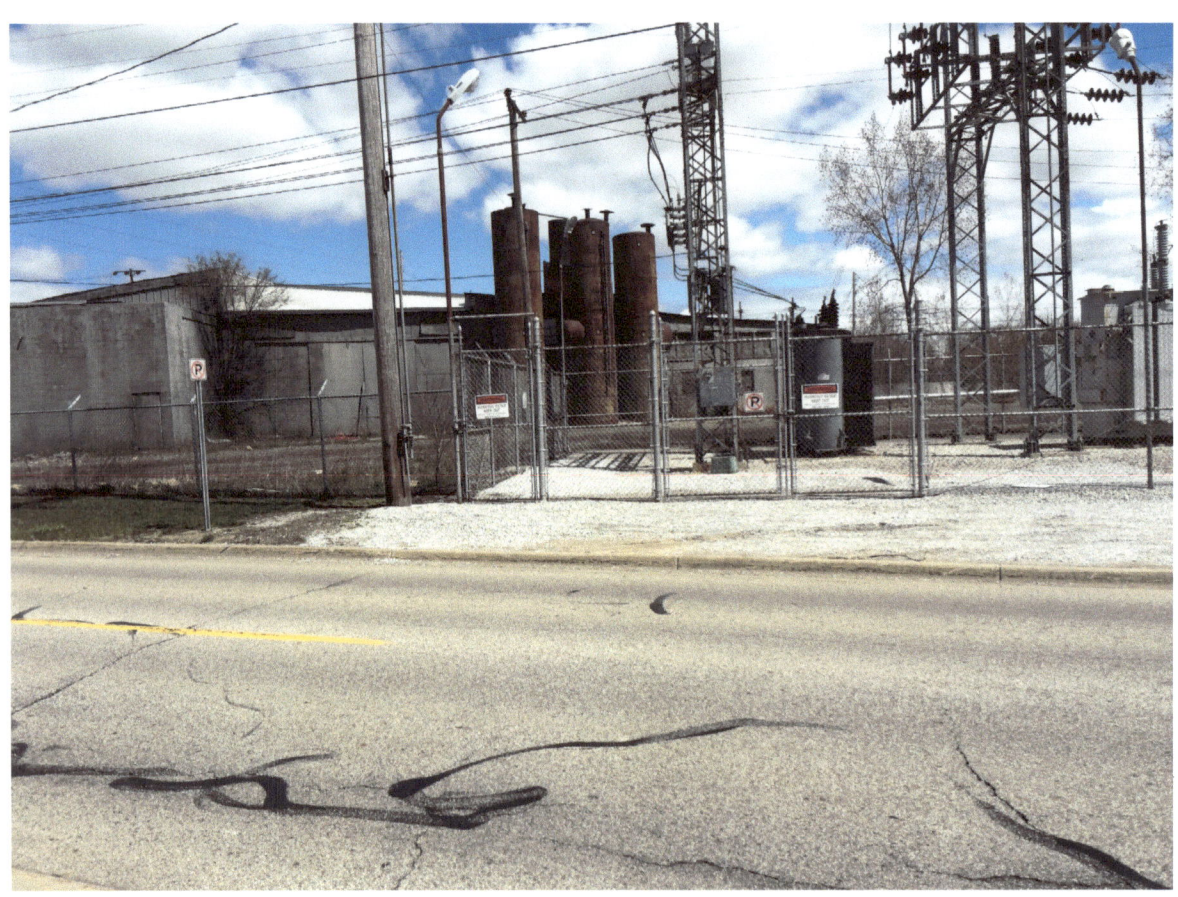

do I have the power ?
do I have the right?

How will this *end?*

A shadow on the wall?

A claw or a hand ?

Cut me

      Or

          Hold me?

What is the answer ?

My son, Cameron
My legacy?

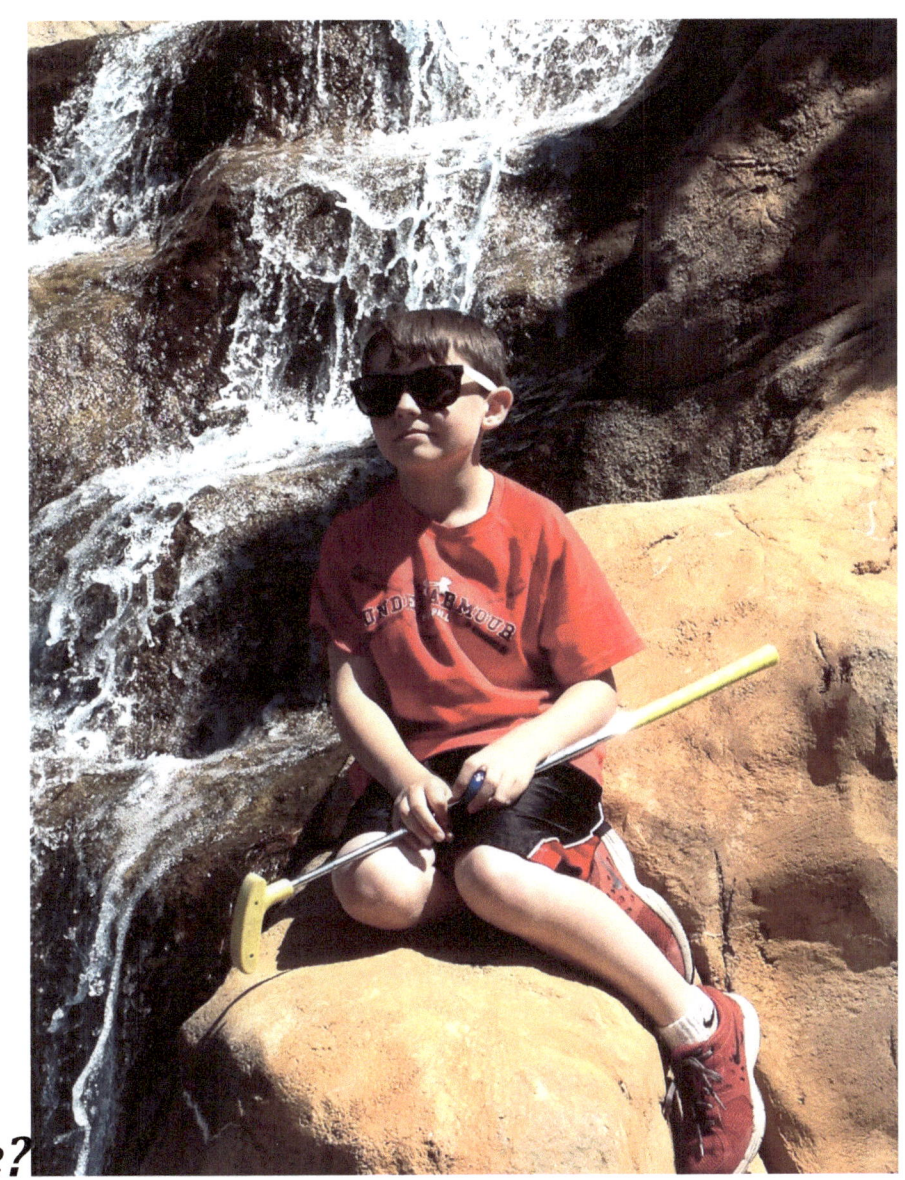

This one?

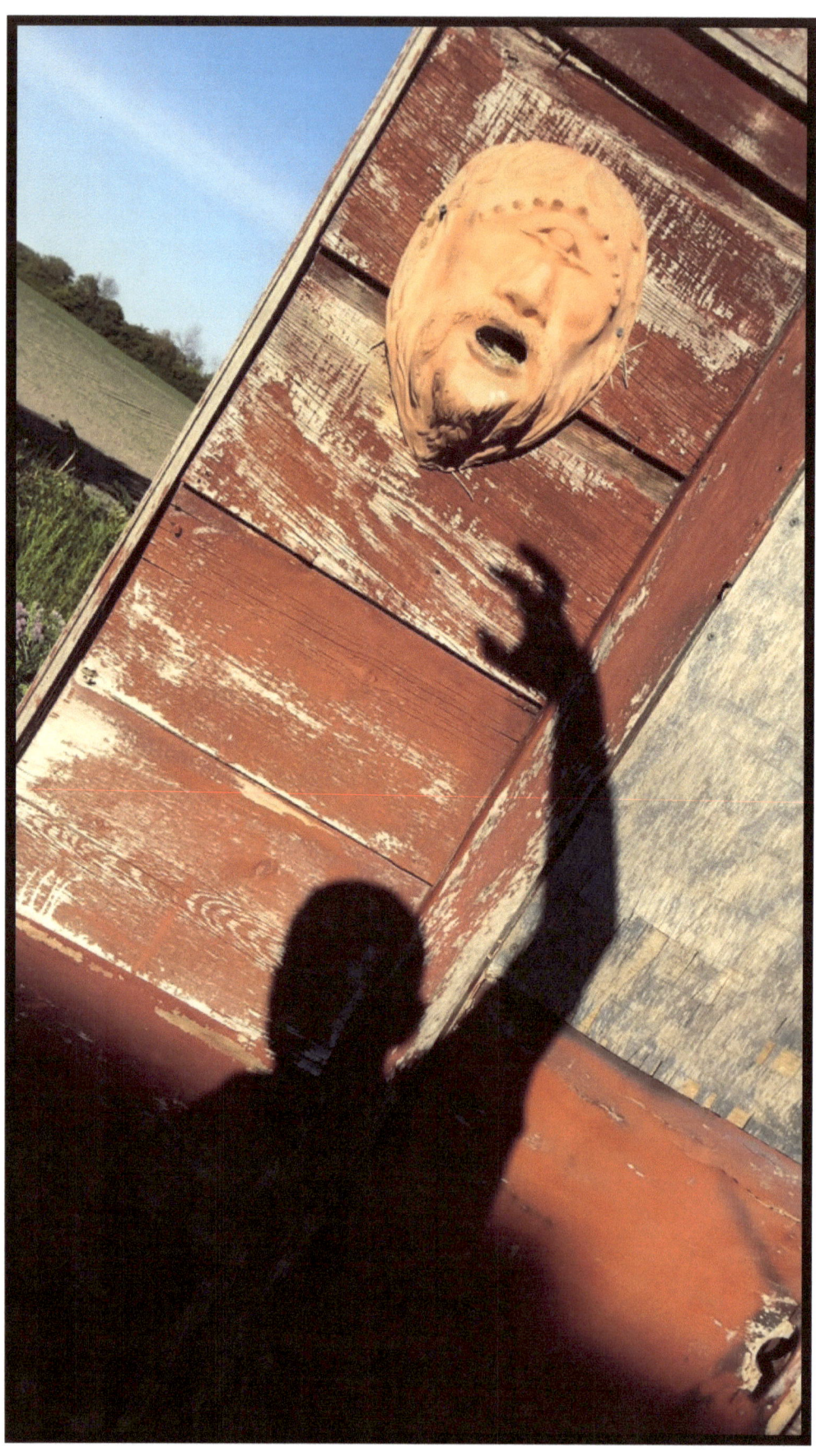